THE
UNWRITTEN
RULES

THE UNWRITTEN RULES

LEADERSHIP IN THE WORK PLACE

GUY P FEHR, RPA, FMP

AuthorHouse™ LLC
1663 Liberty Drive
Bloomington, IN 47403
www.authorhouse.com
Phone: 1-800-839-8640

Published by AuthorHouse   06/12/2014

ISBN: 978-1-4969-1838-3 (sc)
ISBN: 978-1-4969-1837-6 (e)

There are unwritten rules in every workplace that managers should keep in mind during their day to day activities. If these unwritten rules are not understood or ignored, the results can include low morale, high costs, unhappy clients, low productivity, haphazard work, poor teamwork, distrust, costly disfunction, excessive absenteeism and the list goes on.

From your first day as a manager and every day after, your effectiveness as a leader in the workplace hinges on your awareness of, and adherance to the unwritten rules. Managers unknowingly cause problems amongst their staff or defeat themselves everyday because they are either not aware of, or ignoring one or more of these unwritten rules.

"The Unwritten Rules" identifies some of the most common errors made by managers; issues not normally found in leadership development programs. Whether you are a seasoned manager or a new manager, if you are struggling with issues like those listed above; take heart, these are just symptoms that can be addressed. This book is for you!

I dedicate this book
to my two sons,
Garnet and Garrison.
Both natural leaders.

CONTENTS

Introduction...xi

Points of Context xvii

#1.   Make No Changes for Six Months 1

#2.   No Surprises for Your Boss 5

#3.   Don't Bite Red & Whites 7

#4.   Sleep On It 15

#5.   Show Your "Calm" 19

#6.   Beware of Side Deals 27

#7.   Establish Realistic Goals...............................31

#8.   Be the Leader.....................................37

#9.   Work Your Attitude 45

#10. Get to Know Your Teams 51

#11. Be Accessible to Your Staff.......................55

#12. Don't Butt Heads with Culture 57

#13. Don't Solve Problems Yourself 67

#14. Work With the Union 73

#15. Check Your Ego at the Door.....................81

#16. Don't Take Things Personally 87

#17. Assume Connections Exist 93

#18. Place Trust First..97

#19. Own Your Job 103

#20. Forget the 40-Hour Work Week.....................109

Summary 113

About the Author 117

INTRODUCTION

There are unwritten rules in every workplace. You won't find them in policy or procedure manuals or job descriptions, yet they directly impact the success and effectiveness of every manager or supervisor.

These unwritten rules exist in every company or organization; ways to think, things to do, or not to do, and things to watch for or be aware of. They are not spelled out however, so unless you are fortunate enough to have, or have had a savvy mentor, the unwritten rules are usually learned the hard way, after they have been broken or ignored. Unwritten rules will vary to some degree from company to company, and organization to organization, but those listed in this book are fairly consistent everywhere.

As a rule, managers are promoted or hired because it is thought they know or can do the job. But even with all the experience and know-how they might bring with them, these same managers often end up struggling with issues like a drop in productivity or an increase in absenteeism. Moral amongst the staff goes down and the number of grievances goes up. Communications become strained and the manager feels the pressure.

He will push himself, and likely others, in addressing these concerns when the truth is, these issues and many others are just symptoms of another ailment! As in the law of cause and effect, they are the effect, but not the cause. Without exception, they are a result; symptoms that one or more of these unwritten rules have not been, or are not being followed.

As manager, you can spend all kinds of time and energy dealing with the symptoms; or you can look for the cause. The best place to start looking is in the unwritten rules.

You might consider this book your personal pocket mentor. Having said that, you must also know there are literally thousands of volumes written on all aspects of leadership and management and the premises in this book just touch the surface of these powerful topics. However, if you are in a position where you influence or direct the actions of others, then you are in a leadership role and this book is for you.

The intent of this book is to assist you as a manager or supervisor, whether you are experienced or not, by pointing out the unwritten rules and their importance, thus enabling you to see things from a different perspective; and helping you avoid making the same kind of mistakes I have seen happen over and over again, and some I've made myself…

In the last forty years I have worked for mines, railroads, manufacturing, shipping, sales, warehousing, in hospitality and in tourism. I've worked as a human resource and in Human Resources. I've been trainee and trainer many times. I've worked in different areas of the private sector, different levels and branches of government, different shifts, different cities, and trust me, many different environments. I've been a laborer, a tradesman, a supervisor, a warehouseman, a salesman, a coordinator, a consultant, a manager, a director, and an owner.

The experience I draw on to write this book ranges from working midnight shifts as a laborer to overseeing the maintenance and operations of a five million square foot portfolio; from the teamwork of heavy labor to the teamwork of administration; from planning a shift to multi-year strategic planning; and working with people from all walks of life. I have experience in unionized and non-unionized environments; and have managed staff spread across different cities.

Now having a diverse background is certainly no claim to fame. I only share my background as a reference to the variety of people, professions, organizations and situations I have found myself in and in each scenario, I have seen these unwritten rules both applied and ignored, and seen the results of each approach. These are things that don't show up in any company management manual, but they are every bit as important as managing a budget, following a schedule, or sticking to policy.

"One can go to school on bad examples"

What follows are those lessons I've learned from supervisors, managers, and coworkers over the years. Not learned in the normal sense of the word, for while many of these folks were absolutely excellent, some were challenging and frankly, others were simply terrible to work for. But I learned early in life, one can go to school on bad examples as well as good. The rules I share with you here are the most valuable lessons I have learned from the excellent to the terrible and everything in between.

To put it another way, I've been down the management road many times, and if I do have a claim to fame, it's that I can point out to others, especially new managers, where the pot holes are and how best to avoid them. Many times, I have helped others settle into new roles as managers or supervisors. As they've worked their way through challenges, I've been able to provide them with alternate perspectives to consider, different approaches to try and mind sets to adopt that have made a positive difference.

If you are an experienced manager, kudos to you for perusing this book. I'm certain you will find your workplace in its pages. If you are new to management and have just received a promotion, congrats. If you were a supervisor before and now you are a manager, trust me, you are still a supervisor in many respects even though the scale of your responsibility has changed.

What you need to keep in mind as you read this book is, all career paths have potholes and they are easy to hit, especially with tight deadlines, conflicting priorities, fiscal restraint, cross functional teams, union/management relationships, and all the other realities of management. A few of these potholes are deep enough to throw you off the road, if you know what I mean, whereas others just make the ride uncomfortable and progress slow. This little book will show you how to avoid the potholes most often hit by managers and supervisors.

I was recently invited to meet with some Organizational Development Consultants to provide input and share my thoughts regarding a development program for new managers. They were interested in what I would suggest be incorporated into a management development program. They asked a number of questions and took a lot of notes; and I could tell some of the things I pointed out, not only surprised them, but rang true to them as well. The seed of an idea for this "manager's guide book" took root during that meeting.

Some of the concepts I shared with those consultants are the same as the advice in this book. And the advice in this book is the same stuff I've been sharing with new supervisors and managers for the last twenty-five years. I know your time is valuable so I've tried to keep things to the point and only used examples to illustrate where I think it would be beneficial. Like a good burger, my intent for this book is to be all meat and no filler, so enjoy.

POINTS OF CONTEXT

Before we get started, I need to make two quick points.

These rules aren't really rules in the strictest sense of the word, but powerful and effective guidelines, or ways of thinking that will aid a supervisor or manager. For simplicity sake though, I like to refer to them as rules because like all rules, there is a penalty for breaking them. If you are a new supervisor or manager, these will help you. If you've been a manager for a while and are having difficulties, there is a good chance you may be overlooking one of these rules or perhaps aren't giving them the attention they require. And if being promoted to a supervisor or manager is something you have set your sites on, and you want to be seen as a prime candidate, well these rules will benefit you as well.

These rules are not in any specific order. As much as it would simplify things by giving these rules an order of importance, it would be impossible. They are all both separate and interlinked. What is more, each workplace and scenario has differences driving the importance of one over another. They are all important and each rule is connected to or supports the others in some way. You are welcome to attach importance to them in whatever order suits you, or your workplace. They are just listed here in what seems a logical sequence.

RULE # 1

MAKE NO CHANGES FOR SIX MONTHS

Tell yourself this long before you begin your first day. If you are tempted to step into your new job and make changes right off the bat, beware! This may be a huge mistake you find yourself scrambling to correct later.

You see, during your first six months you will have a number of epiphanies; moments where it comes to you, "Oh, so that's why…. I wondered about that." Some of these are big and some are small, but they all add up to a broader understanding of your organization and the history behind things. Your "big picture" needs time to fill in. It is far more prudent to first take the time to understand why things are the way they are, than to initiating change right off the bat. For most midsized and larger organizations, this big picture view will be starting to fill in nicely around the six month point.

There are two possible situations that have moved you into management. Either you have been promoted from within and know the workplace well, or you have accepted a position with a new company and have the organization and workplace to learn. This rule applies to both.

Those that are promoted from within might think, "If I have already worked here for years and know what needs to be changed, why shouldn't I change it right away, now that I'm manager?"

My answer is simple and I'll admit there is a chance it doesn't universally apply, but the reality is, the moment you are in charge, the moment you assume and fully understand your new responsibilities, you will go through some paradigm shifts. You begin to see things through different lenses than you used to.

These lenses have labels like budget, productivity, strategic direction, culture, politics, morale, work-flow, relationships and processes. At first these lenses might seem perfectly clear, but time polishes them to reveal aspects missed initially. After a few months in the new role and sitting in on various meetings, they begin to clear up.

Why six months? Well this might vary a little based on you and the company you work for, but I say six months mostly to drive the point home. I've found six months works, but the actual time-lines have to be your decision based on your situation. At the very least, hold off making any big changes until your feeling of strangeness for the new workplace or your new role is waning and things are beginning to normalize for you. If at this point you see a change needs to be made, go for it. That's why you are being paid.

Remember, as a new manager, you and your new staff will already feel the change of you being there. There will be those that will simply wonder what to expect, and others will hope to influence you in some direction or another. This is just human nature in the workplace, so be ready for it and consider carefully the input you receive.

The exceptions... There are obviously exceptions to this rule and I would be remiss if I didn't identify them. If you were hired specifically to bring about a change, or your new boss is directing you to make a specific change now! You don't have a lot of choice. But learn as much as you can about the change and its impact, so you can speak to its ramifications if necessary. And if a situation is unsafe, you need to act the moment you are aware of it. Change what you have to, to make it safe.

RULE # 2

No Surprises for Your Boss

The best way to understand this rule is to imagine your boss questioning you in front of others, regarding something that happened in your department, and you know nothing about it. He apparently knows more about it than you do. It doesn't quite feel like you've got your fingers on the pulse of your department, does it. At a moment like this, an initial heads-up from your staff would have done two things for you. It would have informed and/or involved you. You would have been able to respond to your boss's questions knowledgeably.

Now, imagine yourself in your boss's position. When things happen (and they do), give your boss a heads-up. This can be a quick phone call, a text, or an email if you know he's in the office and will get it right away.

Even if you don't really know too much yet, make him aware something's going on., i.e. "...We just had a sprinkler head snap off and it's caused a lot of water damage. I'm headed over there now to assess. I'll update you when I know more." Or, "...Just an FYI, the Fire inspector is going to be here on Thursday." Or, "... I just had a meeting with

Sharon from finance and she's concerned about signing authorities. I expect you'll be getting a call from her."

Keeping your boss in the loop, also keeps them in a position to help you, especially if you have made a mistake. They will likely have fixes available that you haven't thought of or aren't aware of. It's all about enabling them to make informed decisions. It lets them know when you need them to run interference for you or your team, and it gives them the opportunity to mentor you through a variety of scenarios.

At the end of the day, good news or bad, your boss will always appreciate timely info.

RULE # 3
DON'T BITE RED & WHITES

Anybody that's fished has likely seen a red and white spoon or fishing lure, and a "Red &White" is just my term for those situations where you are best to keep your thoughts or opinions to yourself; or in other words, don't bite the hook dangled in front of you. Of course the real key here is recognizing the temptation; recognizing the red and white spoon for what it is and don't take the bait.

Admittedly, this is a lot easier said than done; and hind sight is usually our best teacher. Almost everyone, at one time or another has experienced the feeling of being caught and pulled in a direction they hadn't planned on and certainly didn't want to go, just for making the wrong comment.

But for those rare individuals out there that haven't experienced this feeling, here is how you might recognize a red and white spoon.

If you feel strongly about a situation and want to respond hard and fast, recognize this is a flag to stop and think. When you feel so compelled, forethought and strategy are your friends. Ask yourself:

What are your options and where might each of them take you?

➢ What direction would you like the conversation to go?
➢ What options get you there?
➢ What impression do you want to leave?
➢ Is it really worth getting upset over?
➢ What's really important?

Think about your possible responses, or the direction the conversation might go and you'll begin to see the dangers of;

➢ how you might get drawn into an argument,
➢ finding yourself defending someone else's position,
➢ making the regrettable "snap decision" that turns out to be wrong later,
➢ getting bogged down arguing a minor point when the big picture is where your focus should be,
➢ saying something thoughtless and having to apologize for it later.

Hind-sight easily shows these "Red & Whites" for what they were, but to recognize them before you bite, that's the trick!

"Men and fish are alike. They both get into trouble when they open their mouths".
~Author Unknown~

You should also be aware not all "Red & Whites" come at you with strong emotions attached. Some situations may be innocent enough in how they come about, but the end result can be shocking. Here are a few examples.

Gender issues are definitely in this category. Regardless whether you are a man or a woman, you will encounter gender scenarios in the workplace where a thoughtless (sometimes not so thoughtless), comment can land you in hot water.

Those jokey comments with sexual double-meanings are probably the most obvious examples here. As a manager, a supervisor, and a coworker, avoid initiating these kinds of interactions and recognize the dangers of joining in. What one person might view as a harmless joke can be very offensive to another. And once you've offended someone, things can go south very quickly.

Oh and don't assume that because someone else gets away with saying things, you will too. I worked with a guy that had just the right mix of style and humor to get the intended laugh, and he got away with amusingly shocking comments to female coworkers. Had any one of the hundreds of other guys on site said the same things (including me), they would have came across as inappropriate.

Choosing the wrong battle is also like taking on a red and white spoon. It might feel righteous but it likely won't end as satisfactorily as you hope.

For example, I once had an administrative staff member complain to me about some calendars she'd seen through the open doorway on the far wall of the maintenance shop. They were tool calendars given out by suppliers with pictures of women in bathing suits holding pipe wrenches and other tools. Offended by this exploitation of women, she insisted they were inappropriate and be removed. I had a talk with the maintenance guys and the calendars disappeared.

Later that week, I walked past her cubicle and her screen-saver was one of those "Firemen" screen-savers, where they are posing with their coveralls half off. They weren't trying to sell tools, they were selling screen-savers! As I looked around there were a number of screen savers like this on the floor in the cubicles all around hers.

Now I know what you're thinking, and the double standard made it oh-so-tempting to have all the screen-savers go the way of the calendar.

Thinking this through, I recognized the red and white spoon before me. I needed to work along side these ladies, and I certainly valued their cooperation and support. I couldn't raise the issue with the one without impacting all the others. By forcing the issue I'd have been creating an issue. I'd have won the battle but perhaps lost the war. At the end of the day, it was just a calendar.

Red and white spoons often present themselves when people are agitated; when communications aren't clear. When, in their agitated state, they see only a couple options which they present to you, their manager and expect a decision. Heads-up! This is often a lose/lose scenario. Each option will likely have a down side, simply because the people bringing them to you are emotionally charged.

When you are faced with just two choices where going either way will cause a problem; and if a call needs to be made, make it knowingly. But if a call doesn't need to be made at that moment, take the time to look for more options where everyone benefits, or at least the losses are minimized.

Another example might be when an employee might make a request that, on the surface seems reasonable, but agreement from you sets a precedent that will be difficult or costly to repeat.

I once joined an organization where an employee presented me with, what I thought was a fairly justifiable reason to buy him some work-boots. I'd bought hundreds of pairs of work boots with previous companies and actually thought nothing of it. But I was new to this particular organization and still well within the first six months, so I told him I'd look into it.

When I mentioned the request to my boss, his straight-faced, but exaggerated answer was, *"The first pair of boots you buy will cost a million dollars."*

Turns out this had been an ongoing and yet to be resolved issue with this organization affecting many properties and employees. As the newest manager, having only been there a couple months, it certainly wasn't my issue to resolve by setting a precedent at that point in time.

So, if someone says something that is just begging for an argument, don't bite! If one of your staff chooses to make a stand and draws the proverbial line in the sand in front of others, don't bite! (You can always deal with him later away from his friends.) If this happens too often, expose the "Red & White" to those he's chosen as his audience by saying something like, "Why do you always draw a line in the sand like that when you know how easily it can be messed up? Or why would you make statements like that, as if anyone is arguing with you? And then earnestly listen to his answers! That's the key to sorting things out. (See rule 16.)

A particularly nasty red & white is hearsay. Hearsay acted upon without checking it out yourself first, can do damage to your reputation, to moral, and to your team.

Always confirm with the individual referred to before taking any action or for that matter locking in on an opinion yourself. Regardless what you are told by others about your staff, i.e. he said this or they did that; there is always more to learn by talking to the individual(s) yourself. Always give your staff the benefit of the doubt until they remove the doubt themselves. You may have heard this before in the form of, "*innocent until proven guilty*".

Sometimes what you learn by talking with the individual(s) confirms what you heard and you have a clear course of action. On the other hand, an additional detail or two can change a scenario completely.

The key here is to be sure, to check out the details, and to hear both or all sides. This little bit of common sense can sometimes get lost in the heat of a moment and lead to a wrong "snap decision".

And last but certainly not least; the most common red and white out there is that email you get that riles you up and prompts you to hammer out that perfectly worded response that deftly put that person in their place with all the precision of a linguistics professor, and you actually feel satisfaction sitting there at your desk just typing it out...

You know what I'm talking about. Rule of thumb here is, if you're angry, don't send it. In fact, take their name out of the send field, so you can't accidentally send it. (*Guess how I learned this lesson.*) Tomorrow if you are still upset, still don't send it.

When you are no longer upset, don't even try to edit the vitriol out of it. Erase it and start over, or better yet, go see the person if you can. Over 90% of our communication is tone and expression. The words in email equal only 7% of full, in person communication. How easy it is to be misunderstood. When resolving an issue, face to face is best.

(For more insight into recognizing "Red & Whites" also see Rule 15.)

RULE #4

SLEEP ON IT

This rule is so closely related to not biting red and white spoons that it had to come next. This is all about reactionary decisions.

Time and time again, new managers find themselves having to deal with the negative effects of reactionary decisions. Embarrassed by the 20:20 vision of hindsight, they either have to live with their mistake or invest time and energy (and sometimes funds) into cleaning it up.

You won't always have the option of mulling over the best course of action but when you do, exercise your option. Take the time to think it through. Be careful though, don't apply this rule to every scenario, or take too long with the ones you do, or you will soon be seen as indecisive. (*See "Own Your Job".*)

What I am talking about here are things like resource planning, process or program changes, and disciplinary situations.

Resource planning is often seen as pretty straight forward; i.e. matching jobs to individuals. But once you add succession planning and learning opportunity to the factors, A little more thought often pays off.

Process or program changes are always best thought out clearly and discussed with those involved. No snap decisions here.

Disciplinary decisions, in my experience, are always better and more effective after a little more water has flowed under the bridge.

"Things will look better in the morning."

My grandfather used to say, "Things will look different in the morning." As a homesteading farmer in the early 1900's, he couldn't have been farther from the corporate world of today or any closer to the truth. Allowing ourselves the time to make some decisions enables greater clarity and objectivity.

Even when presented with proposals they see merit in, upper management will often say something along the lines of, *"Let me think about it."* or, *"Can I get back to you in a couple days?"* What they're wisely doing is giving themselves the time to examine the proposal for its fit into the big picture and any future ramifications that may result. They may consult with a few others as well, so that when they do come back with a decision, they are able to paint a clear picture for you as to why or why not.

So when things happen (and they do), and changes need to be made (and they will), giving yourself a little time will enable a better thought out decision that will pay off and be appreciated by those around you.

"Be willing to make decisions. That's the most important quality in a good leader. Don't fall victim to what I call the Ready Aim-Aim-Aim Syndrome. You must be willing to fire."
~T. Boone Pickens~

Keeping with Mr. Pickens' comparison of "Ready Aim Fire" to making leadership decisions, I would suggest, making a reactionary or snap decisions is a bit like firing, seeing what you hit, and then having to repair the damage or apologize, or both.

RULE #5
SHOW YOUR "CALM"

I was two weeks into a new position as a Facilities Manager, when the water main burst under the basement floor of one of the office buildings in my portfolio. The water pressure heaved the concrete basement floor up fourteen inches before it burst through and flooded a ten thousand square foot labyrinth of meeting rooms and tenant storage rooms full of confidential and legal documents.

Within a few months, the lower level was once again fully renewed into prime office space, conference rooms, and storage rooms. Then a cloud burst full of rain and hail hit the building and a cast iron rain water leader (*A pipe in the ceiling space above the ceiling tiles*) in the lower level snapped under the thermal shock, and flooded the lower level once again.

So there I was Saturday night, second time in less than a year, wading through the halls in the lower level, talking with my staff and making sure they had everything they needed for the all-night clean-up.

The supervisor of the crew asked me, "How do you do stay so calm when this place keeps flooding?"

I was a little surprised by her question and responded with, "What's to get excited about? You have enough staff, you have the tools you need and you all know what needs to be done. Everything that can be done is being done."

I share this example to illustrate how your reactions to events are noted by your staff. If they see you as calm, in what might otherwise be a stressful situation, it does two things. It bolsters their confidence in your ability to lead and deal with not only the situation at hand, but others as well. It can also send the message that you are also confident in them.

People have more confidence in a leader that remains calm; than in a leader that gets excited easily or is quick to anger. I'm not referring to just those that report to you, but those that work alongside you, and those you report to as well. This is so important a trait to develop that I regularly introduce this concept to entry level applicants during interviews. I talk about how valuable an employee is that can keep his head when everyone is loosing it around them, whether those around them are co-workers or clients.

While it doesn't need to be said that everyone benefits from self control. What does need to be pointed out is your staff and coworkers know the stresses of the workplace and your self control is seen as competence.

Taking this a step further; watch that you don't wear your responsibilities on your face either. Easier said than done? Definitely! But here's the trick. Don't label your responsibilities with negative terms, especially to yourself. If you tag them as being a never ending curse, ridiculous, impossible to achieve, stupid, pointless, imprisoning, etc., these thoughts will affect how you work, how you walk, how you talk, and how you look. Over time, they will affect how you eat and sleep as well.

Instead, find positive terms like; well worth doing, money saving, done for the good of others, enabling, supportive of corporate direction, bringing closure, something you're good at, a crucial part of being part of something much bigger than yourself. This internal adjustment of your inward point of view will seep into every aspect of your behavior and outward appearance.

> **"In any contest between power and patience, bet on patience."**
>
> **~Anonymous~**

It's very important here to stress that I'm not talking about feigning calmness for the benefit of others, but being truly calm. To get to and maintain this state is all about putting things in perspective and keeping them there. It is about taking control of your thoughts rather than letting them control you.

This is easier when you enable yourself to be at your best at work and know when you aren't. There are innumerable things that can affect our behavior at work; the amount of sleep we get, the sports we play, trying to quit smoking, dieting, personal relationship issues, organizational change... The point is, "they affect our performance! They affect our calm.

Most of us know when we are not at our best at work. Personally, I know if I haven't had enough sleep, I'm a different guy at work than when I'm rested. To use the poker term, I recognize my own "tells," and when I do, I make a point of getting the rest I need.

When you know what your "tells" are, you are better able to address them. They might be:

➢ irritability,
➢ sarcasm
➢ anxiousness,
➢ distractedness
➢ worry,
➢ impatience
➢ insecurity,
➢ jealousy,
➢ envy,

➢ stubbornness,
➢ speaking without thinking,
➢ being offended easily

Things like anxiety, worry, and jealousy tend to inhibit good judgment and have the effect of making problems look bigger. Continued anxiety or worry is demoralizing. We each need to recognize what impacts our performance at work and what our own "tells" are in order to make the necessary changes if possible or at the very least maintain control of our thoughts.

> **"Problems can often go away by looking at them differently."**

Sometimes a shift in perspective can bring about a profound change. I know a fellow whose fuse always used to be half lit, and he would turn red, get mad, and blow up at the slightest irritation or verbal challenges. A situation would make him irritable and he would still be irritable long after it was over. Just recalling it would raise his ire.

Then one day, he changed. He was relaxed, calm, and amazingly not aggravated by the things that used to get him wound up. In meetings with clients, where decisions were questioned and plans were established, he fielded every question with diplomacy and eloquence. If he didn't know an answer, he confidently admitted it. He was decisive and accommodating and every aspect of his demeanor spoke of poise and professionalism.

It was such a significant change I had to ask him what happened, as he didn't seem bothered by things any more.

He told me, "I realized that everything on my plate six months ago has come to pass. And in six months I will have different issues to deal with than I do right now. Everything comes to pass. So why get wound up?"

That was it! He had found a way to put things in a perspective that enabled him to take things in stride and deal with them without breaking a sweat.

"Everything comes to pass, so why get wound up?" What a profound realization. Calmness is a foundational characteristic of leadership. I don't think this simple change in perspective made him a better leader, but it certainly enabled others to see the competent leader he was.

Another manager I know has had a very close brush with his own mortality. Do you think work issues get him stressed? Not hardly. His measure of what's worth getting stressed about is on a far bigger scale than the rest of us.

The last tip I'll share on managing your perspective is to play the "what if" game. Ask yourself, "What if this happens?" or "What if that happens?" Pick those things that would really create an emergency situation. And then answer your own questions. Go through in your mind, each of the steps that will need to be taken. See yourself solving the problem. Consider what resources you will need and see your self directing their activities.

Going through this mental exercise is like practice as if it really happened, and this mental practice files itself away the same as a real experience; to be called upon should that scenario actually happen. If you can envision yourself calmly handling calamity and challenges; if you see yourself as being calm, you will be.

"Most emergencies aren't emergencies but a simple call to action."

Now some will say, "What about when this happens, or if that happens?"

To them I say it makes no difference. It may seem like the sky is falling for the other person on the phone, but most emergencies aren't emergencies but a simple call to action, which you will have to prioritize appropriately. Some perceived emergencies are based on a lack of understanding which you will need to clarify. For those few real emergencies that come up; if your team is prepared, trained, and knows what needs to be done; they will be handled. In 35 years, I have never seen a team fail to step up to the plate when needed.

So things are going to happen. Count on it, and deal with them as you have to, but keep in mind all the difficulties that challenge you now as a manager are the experiences you will reference in the future. Challenges and difficulties are necessary to your development as a leader.

So take control of your thoughts and your words and actions will follow suit. With practice, calmness will become your default. Remember, you never have more power than when you are perceived as calm.

RULE #6

BEWARE OF SIDE DEALS

It's important to differentiate here between agreements and side deals. Agreements between Supervisors, Managers and Directors of different departments are what make functional organizations. They are a reality and a necessity. Side Deals on the other hand, are those arrangements that wouldn't fare well under scrutiny.

When it comes to side deals between a Supervisor or a Manager and their employees, the unwritten rule is "Don't make-em!"

It's a rare side deal that doesn't come back to haunt you or your successor. These things might seem like a workable solution at the time, but in one way or another, someone always end up paying or has to clean things up later, and this someone is usually the manager. I'm talking specifically here, about things that don't show up on a time sheet, that go undocumented, or that might get documented when they shouldn't be.

In a unionized workplace, some examples might be a manager that turns a blind eye to his most dependable supervisor using the company vehicle as his own; or when a manager suggests to an employee that has put in a few extra hours, *"Tell you what, you can go home at noon tomorrow and take Friday off as well. We just won't put any overtime on the time sheets. "wink!"*

At one place I worked, I came back from vacation to hear my boss make this arrangement with one of the staff that reported to me, and when I asked him why he did it, he was pleased as punch that he had staved off a grievance. (Apparently he had asked the wrong man to work some overtime.) He proudly told me that he had never had a grievance in 10 years. And at that point, I knew why. A few weeks later, that same employee asked me for another day off in exchange for more unauthorized overtime he was willing to work. He felt comfortable enough to suggest, *"I'll just fill out my time sheet as if I were here."*

Of course I declined his offer, and gave him a dozen reasons why. He told me that other supervisors in the place did it, but I never gave in.

Years later, after I had moved on from the place, I heard from a reliable source that the employees in that place had such control, that when they all went through a job review process to ensure they were paid commensurate with the value of the duties they performed, the end result was some of the employees ended up making more than their supervisors, and the manager had signed off on this, just before he retired.

In a non-unionized place, some side deals to come back and haunt you might be bonuses in the form of un-earned commissions, or one employee always gets the gravy run in exchange for favors for the boss. I've seen some employees get the green light to take home left over carpet and furnishings from tenant renovations, and other employees get denied.

Let's say one of your staff, asks if they can come in late or leave early the next few days, because of a personal issue at home, and offers to come in on the weekend to make up the hours. There are lots of reasons why I personally would like to say yes to this request, but I don't. This side deal is a red and white spoon and the result of saying yes can be anarchy.

I'll explain. If you say yes, just know there is a high likelihood this request will come at you again and again until the practice of "making up time" will become the norm. It's doubly hard to say no after the precedent has been set. If this practice becomes the norm, then normal office hours loose their importance for this individual, and you as the manager have to add to your duties, more stringent monitoring of this employee's hours and productivity. This is a lot easier to do when everybody works the same hours.

You should also know, other employees will learn the arrangement and come to you with the same request. I mean you did it for one…

If you say no, they may miss a few hours pay, or utilize a few hours vacation to cover off the time, but they will be motivated to address the issue that is interfering with work.

If you work in a unionized environment, the Collective Bargaining Agreement (CBA) may have language for temporary shift changes of this type. If so, then there are proper steps to follow. It's been my experience however, that if you agree to an arrangement like this, you are probably in contravention of the CBA, as they tend to shy away from employees negotiating flexible shifts for themselves.

At the end of the day, whether it is a unionized or non-unionized workplace, the first time you find yourself faced with some kind of a side deal with one or two employees, consider how you might be painting yourself into a corner. Depending on who's on the outside looking in, side deals might be perceived as deception, vulnerability, unfairness, discrimination, a misuse of assets or resources, theft, favoritism, weakness, manipulation, game playing, fraud, and a host of other negative descriptors.

RULE # 7

Establish Realistic Goals

As a manager in a normally paced organization, here is your reality. You will always have things that need doing, and you will always have interruptions. The job ad for your position might have described your position with a phrase like, "…multiple and often conflicting priorities in a fast paced environment."

On more than one occasion, I have heard managers express frustration over not being able to get the things done they personally want to, because they are constantly called on to "be there" for others. They planned on having something done by Tuesday and here it is Thursday and they're still not done.

My advice to them is the same thing I am telling you here. Get in the habit of setting just a few (sometimes maybe just one), weekly goals for your self. Trying to fit a personal goal into just one day of multiple and often conflicting priorities can be a lot harder than it sounds.

So set yourself up to succeed with a few simple strategies.

The first thing you need to do is take control of your scheduler. Block out times for yourself. This is preferable to declining a meeting invite, when the inviter has already checked your scheduler to see when you are available. I have regular times set aside in my scheduler for just this reason, and only my closest coworkers and supervisor know about these times. If you need some prep time for a meeting, add that to your scheduler when you book the meeting or accept the meeting invite.

If you still like the idea of setting daily goals for yourself, there's certainly nothing wrong with this. Just know, there will be days when unplanned things will consume your whole day, so be ready to work late or shift your daily goal forward. I'm talking about meetings, travel, follow-up, and administrivia of all sorts. That's just the job and it will move your plans around. If things really build up and you are just swamped, let your supervisor know, and he/she can help you prioritize. (*See "No surprises for the Boss."*)

A past co-worker (Bob) experienced first hand the frustration of setting unrealistic goals for himself. Bob was no stranger to the organization and I touched base with him a couple times a week after he was promoted to manager. After about five weeks, he expressed his frustration with the inability to get "his" things done.

Bob was setting daily tasks for himself and planning to do this and that, but his days were filled with traveling to and from meetings, and responding to day to day issues from clients, staff and contractors. Even his boss was frustrating him with last minute requests and with, what he felt, were unrealistic expectations. He was having a hard time getting the things he wanted done, done!

**"The good thing about cell phones is
you're always connected.
The bad thing about cell phones is
you're always connected."**

Now Bob's situation was a little unique. He had staff in several places across a region so large that the drive between any of the towns and cities ranged from 110 to 150 miles (177 – 240 Km.), and he spent about three days a week on the highway. While on the road, he was in regular contact via cell, with the supervisors that reported to him, his clients, project managers, planners, contractors and his office.

His Mondays were typically 11-hour days; 4 to 5 hours of which, were on the highway. While he was on the road, he easily fielded a couple dozen calls on his cell, most of which required follow-up of some kind. The weekly project and staff meetings held on Mondays, invariably generated a few new tasks of their own.

Now the good thing about cell phones is you're always connected. The bad thing about cell phones is you're always connected. Cell phones enable you to essentially be in two places at once. You're in the office, and you're not. The down side of being so connected is, a high percentage of those cell phone calls will require a commitment of some type, for when you get back to the office.

When Bob got to the office Tuesday morning, Monday's 30+ email waited in his in-box along with Monday's cell phone commitments. And so his weeks went.

So in answer to his frustration, I suggested he focus on the week rather than the day. That he identify just one or two key tasks to complete in a week, and to work them into every gap in the action. If he got them completed early in the week, perfect; then move on to the next item on his to-do list. I also suggested, he block out time each week in his scheduler for himself and so others would see he was unavailable and wouldn't book a meeting without calling him first. These two small changes carved out a little more time for his goals and enabled him a little flexibility in his time with staff and clients.

Now for the experienced managers reading this, there are obviously more strategies that can be applied, like reorganization, delegation, prioritization, managing expectations, better utilization of technology and a host of others, but what my friend needed most right then, was to cut himself a little slack as he "grew into the job".

From his first day he had set the bar higher for himself, than those around him, including his boss; and he was too focused on what he wasn't getting done. He was just a new manager with his own expectations. By the time I left that organization a few years later, his natural leadership abilities and skills as a manager were honed to the point where he was filling in for his director on a regular basis.

One of the more or less consistent interruptions to your daily work plans will be from your director, who by the very nature of management, will ask for something by a certain date and time. He might shoot you off an email question in 15 seconds or less that will require an hour or more of research just to gather the data needed for the answer.

Let's look now at how an application of this rule might look. Your plate is full, and your boss is asking that you draw up a service contract, or provide feedback on a 50-page proposal, or a personal favorite, "Clear your calendar, you need to be at this meeting."

Remember, the rule here is to establish realistic goals for yourself. If you have already planned to work on another task at this time and attending the meeting will jeopardize completion of that task on time, you need to communicate this. Either let your boss know you have a prior commitment or let your client know about the possible delay.

In other scenario, if you simply can not get something done by the time required, let your boss know why well ahead of time, and she can assist with prioritizing the things on your plate to provide you with the time you need. If there are ramifications to clearing your calendar, she needs to know those as well.

At the end of the day, is it realistic to expect your director to make demands on your time? Absolutely! Just as you do to your supervisors and staff. Is it realistic to let her know when your plate is full? You bet.

And one last thing about goals, regardless of your best planning, things happen. Just deal with things as you have to and recognize, as mentioned before, all the difficulties and challenges you face now form the experience you will look back on as a reference in the future; so keep your head about you. Challenges and difficulties, as mentioned before, are necessary to your development as a leader.

RULE #8

BE THE LEADER

Being an effective communicator is the role of a leader and it is hands down, your most important role as a manager. Whether you are new to the organization or promoted up through the ranks, your staff will be looking to you to fill in the blanks for them.

Whether you've been promoted from within or hired from the outside, your staff expect to see you own your new responsibilities, so forget about still being "one of the guys." That ship has sailed. Your focus needs to be on being there for your staff by being a good manager. Show you still value the positive workplace relationships you've got and that you take your job seriously.

As a new manager, your staff will wonder what they can expect from you. What is going to change? Remember, that as much as things have changed for you by getting this job, things have changed for them as well. If you are new to the organization, they first of all need to know who you are and what you bring to the position. If you are not new to the staff, and they have known you for some time, they will be watching to see if and how the promotion changes you.

Oh, and by the way, so will whomever you report to.

"When I give a man an office, I watch him carefully to see if he is swelling or growing."
~Woodrow Wilson~

You might also keep in mind, the rumour mill can churn out some ridiculous stuff, and never more so than when there's uncertainty; like with a new manager. So I like to start off staff meetings with, "So what rumours have you heard?" This often leads to some great and often amusing discussions, which I always close with my "Rumour Rule of Thumb," which is, "If it seems too bad or too good to be true, it usually is."

This rule, to "Be the Leader" is all about how you see yourself. Your position might be manager but your role is leader. Once you recognize this, your conduct will follow suit. There are dozens of definitions out there differentiating managers from leaders. One says a manager manages things and a leader manages people. Another says a manager gets things done through other people. Another says how leaders empower the people around them to get things done. I think you can see the direction I'm going.

The definition I use is, "If you influence or direct the activities of at least one person, you are a leader." Whether you are a supervisor or a manager, if you have staff, just know you are a leader. You can manage budgets, inventories, schedules, etc., but if you empower your staff and give them the tools they need, you are functioning as a leader.

Some valid questions for managers to ask them selves are:

➢ Do my staff simply take direction or do they follow my lead?

➢ Do I set an example of diligence and reliability; that my staff might emulate?

➢ Do I want my staff merely doing what they're told or thinking about what needs doing without being told?

➢ Do I tell my staff how well or poorly we as a team are doing?

➢ How much autonomy do my staff have?

➢ Do they know the importance of their work?

➢ Do staff share the rumours they've heard?

These questions and many more are a way you keep your fingers on the pulse the team you are leading and your effectiveness as a leader.

I don't dare belabor this too much for there are easily ten thousand other books out there on the various aspects of leadership. This book, remember, is on the unwritten rules that you as a leader, who has likely read some of these other books, still need to know.

"Your greatest success as a manager lies with a focus on being a good leader."

The bottom line is, if you are a manager with a team, you have the option of thinking like a manager or thinking like a leader. Your greatest success as a manager lies with a focus on being a good leader. As that leader, if you develop and empower your staff to the point where they can get on with the job without you, then you are going in the right direction. What you are shooting for is to build up your staff to the point where if an emergency happens or if something totally unexpected comes up, they can deal with it properly without any input from you.

I also need to tell you, that by being a leader, you are guaranteed to upset someone sometime; maybe everyone sometime. Be up front with your staff and tell them you know they will not always like your decisions. That's just the nature of the job. But at the same time tell them you will do your best to help them understand why you've made those decisions.

If you want to make enemies, try to change something.

~Woodrow Wilson~

I suppose one of the easiest and most likely places you will upset folks is when you change the way things are done. As a manager, you should regularly examine your team's processes and methods to see if they are still appropriate.

The status quo may have been exactly what was needed at one time, but time moves on and things change. In fact change is the only constant, and we need to be ready to respond in kind. So when it comes to the status quo, consider it your job to question it. And if changes need to be made, it will never hurt to review rule # 13, "Don't Solve Problems Yourself."

People will look to you for decisions and you should guard against making poorly thought out, snap decisions just as much as you should not defer a decision indefinitely. But when you make a call, right or wrong, own it.

The bigger the issue, the tougher the decision, the more likely it is that some will be upset. Key word here is "some". If you are indecisive or are seen as afraid to make a decision, you will upset "everyone." Always keep in mind, your best employees want a strong leader and your weakest employees need a strong leader.

Listen to your staff. Listening is a common characteristic of excellent leaders. Make no mistake here; listening is a skill everyone can get better at. I'm not just talking about giving them your attention. Along with your attention, listen to hear the message, amongst the words. Think about what you are hearing. If your staff know you are listening, and paying attention to what they are saying, you will learn more from them. On the other side of the coin, if they feel you aren't listening to them, they will stop talking to you.

I once had a Director of a large property management organization say to me, "Buildings are easy, people are difficult." No truer words have ever been said. As complicated as a large multifunctional facility can be, there is still a right way and a wrong way to do everything. The same can't always be said for people.

Since then I have realized this phrase is universally adaptable. i.e. Trucking is easy, people are difficult; or Retail is easy, people are difficult... Computers are easy, people are difficult. Insert the vocation of your choice and see if it doesn't fit.

The fact this statement is so universally adaptable illustrates that a person can know every technical and operational aspect of the job and yet their success as a manager will still hinge on their skills with people. Behavioral competencies like good communication, team building, motivation and recognition are underlying leadership competencies of effective managers. To be sure, technical competencies and operational insight are important for working with things and processes, but these behavioral competencies are the key to working with people. Developing them is key to developing your leadership skills.

As I mentioned at the beginning of this book, I encourage you to explore each and every topic in leadership development and management skills. "Being the leader" is, not relying on your company to develop your leadership skills for you, but to take up this challenge yourself. Check out the library. It is full of leadership material. See if your company has a reference library; many do. If you work with a large organization, ask the human resources department about leadership competency courses and workshops. Get involved in your community. Ask whom ever you report to for opportunities to be involved in projects and programs that will develop leadership competencies.

Whatever you do in this direction will pay off because of one simple fact; **"We are all in the people business!"**

RULE #9
WORK YOUR ATTITUDE

Your attitude influences the attitudes of those around you. So while you can't actually change their attitudes, you can set the tone; so that's where you focus your attention.

This is more than just walking around in a good mood and giving out "Atta Boys" and pats on the back. I'm talking about truly believing in your staff; their value on your team and to the organization.

Your belief in them gives credibility to your expectations. It allows you to be confident in their ability to get the job done without having to tell them how to do it. And they will "get it!" Your staff will pick up on your belief and the level of your confidence in them.

"Your staff will usually live up to or down to your expectations."

Now remember I said your belief gives credibility to your expectations. This goes both ways. If you believe you have a terrible employee, your expectations of his performance will naturally be lower. And there's thing about expectations you need to know; your staff will usually live up to or down to your expectations. In 1968, two researchers named Rosenthal and Jacobsen discovered the link between expectations and performance and dubbed it the "Pygmalion Effect".

"Seeing isn't believing.
Believing is seeing!"

To get things on the right track, you need to examine the story(s) you are telling yourself; what you are believing. You've likely heard the phrase, "Seeing is Believing." Well I'll go on record here and say the opposite is more accurate. "Believing is Seeing" It's a fact that people will weave whatever they see into what they believe.

For example: Let's say I've told myself an individual is lazy and spends his time avoiding work and people. Then one day as I'm approaching, I see him walk quickly away and disappear around a corner. I might think to myself, "Look at that lazy guy. He seen me coming and took off so I wouldn't ask him what he was working on."

Now on the other hand, let's say I've told myself that very same individual is one of my best staff; conscientious and hardworking. Now the same scenario happens where I see him walk quickly away and disappear around a corner as I approached, I might think to myself, "Wow, look at him go. You sure don't see him standing around. He's sure an asset to the team."

"The moment we want to believe something, we suddenly see all the arguments for it, and become blind to the arguments against it."

~George Bernard Shaw~

The best way to work your attitude is to start off by telling yourself the right story. And the first challenge you might have in doing this may well come from the comments of other managers around you; or if you are just starting in a new role, the orientation you receive. I'm referring here to those folks that help you get settled in; your new boss, the previous manager, folks in the office, and any others that take the time to help you by forewarning you about certain individuals.

I don't want to leave you with the wrong impression here. This info is all valuable and 100% accurate according to their beliefs. It is coming your way with the best of intentions. But the recalling of events is often augmented with impressions and opinions. Gaps get filled with assumptions, and you need to filter this "first info" very carefully. Take the time to make up your own mind on things and guard your thoughts.

I say "guard your thoughts" because they will always lead to words and action. As in cause and effect, your thoughts are the cause and your words and actions are the effect. If you embrace the wrong story, you may never see the right one. Good thoughts will never have bad results, and if you share good thoughts with others, you are planting seeds all around you.

> **"Whether they are positive or negative,**
> **Your thoughts are the beginnings**
> **of your results."**

I would be remiss here if I didn't also illustrate the connection between your attitude and beginnings. Consider this. Your job is full of beginnings. Each day has a beginning; so to with each week, month, and year. Each new responsibility, project or process has a beginning. Your relationships with each new employee, new co-worker, new client and new boss have a beginning.

A "right beginning" is one of the most important things you as a manager should strive for and foster amongst your staff. On this note, I personally focus on and look for the right attitude at the interview stage with new employees. I check on aptitude but look for attitude. An aptitude for the job is important but the right attitude is critical. So many times, I have seen people hired for aptitude and fired for attitude. New employees know from day one, what I'm looking for, and that sets the tone for their "right beginning" with the organization.

Another way to work your attitude and avoid undermining your staff's attitude, is by managing your own critical remarks. I'm not referring here to suggestions for improvement or constructive criticism tactfully shared, I'm referring to the damage caused by thoughtlessly venting frustration to the wrong audience. At the end of the day, it has never been an effective use of anyone's time to criticize the inevitable. What's important to you as a new manager is to "not" set yourself up as the one folks could point to as the leader of the critics!

Your job is to solve problems, not create or magnify them; to be a change agent rather than a source of resistance to change; by communicating so your staff understand the issues that affect them. A private discussion with your boss where you might express your concerns is appropriate, whereas outspoken workplace criticism isn't.

**"Confidence is contagious.
So is lack of confidence."**

~ Vince Lombardi~

Whenever you are in a group, think about how contagious you are. Enthusiasm, determination, optimism, and confidence are contagious; unfortunately, so too are cynicism, pessimism, passive aggressiveness, and doubt. Good or bad attitudes are equally infectious and if unchecked, can spread from one to another. Recognize the power your attitude has to halt a negative trend and positively affect the attitudes of others, and then use it.

> **"Whether you believe you can do a thing or not, you are right."**
>
> **~Henry Ford~**

RULE #10

GET TO KNOW YOUR TEAMS

This is pluralized to highlight the fact that you are likely involved with a few teams, the most important of which are the management team you are part of and the team you lead, i.e. the supervisors that report to you and the staff that report to them. Beyond this, consider the leadership team of the company; project teams you're on, and so on.

If you are a new manager, it's going to take you some time to get to know the perspectives of the individuals around you in each of these teams. This understanding however, is necessary for your effective communication and functionality on each team.

Obviously, if you are new to the organization, and have everyone to get to know, this is easier said than done. The easiest and best place to start is with the two perspectives you need to understand first; the perspective of whom you report to, and that of those who report to you.

Understanding the perspectives of the org chart immediately above and below you, will help you understand some of the challenges of the position you're in. This understanding enables better communication and planning. And the environment and culture of your team within the organization will begin to show itself.

Some of the initial things you need to understand about your boss are: how much updating does she want, and about what types of things. How much of the day to day aspects of your job does she understand and what are her expectations of you and the staff you direct? Where are you and she in the organizational structure and how does your department interact with other departments?

From your staff you need to understand how they see themselves and if they see or understand the value and importance of the work they do. What are their expectations of you and how did your predecessor work with them? Are there any things they need from you right away?

As your interactions with the staff fill in the blanks for you, be on full receive, but weigh the info you get on the reasonable scale. If it doesn't sound reasonable, there are likely aspects of the story missing or misconstrued.

The flip side of getting to know your teams is to let them get to know you. In your conversations with your staff, never forget where you came from. Draw on your personal history and experiences to understand and communicate with your supervisors and their crews. If you've worked twelve-hour shifts, there's a part of you that naturally understands your shift workers. If you've done some of the dirtiest of jobs, you can relate with empathy to those that have a dirty job to do. If you've had a terrible boss, don't emulate him. If you've had a great boss, emulate him. You know how it feels to be recognized, so recognize others. If you've been on a great team, be that team mate now. You've been held accountable so hold others accountable as well.

This list can go on and on but the point is, you weren't born the night before you got this job. Use your experience in a tactful manner to keep things real with your staff. Like so many of the unwritten rules, this sounds like common sense, but my experience is "common sense" is sometimes an oxymoron like "petty cash." There's nothing petty about cash, and sense is not always common.

RULE #11

BE ACCESSIBLE TO YOUR STAFF

This rule is right after, "Get to Know Your Teams" for a reason. Being accessible is another way to get to know your staff and your accessibility enables you as a leader to influence the culture of your group or team. You may feel you are doing a great job by being at your desk before anyone else gets there and still at your desk after they leave; but you will be doing a better job by getting out from behind your desk and out on the shop floor. Being visible and accessible will yield positive results, so get out of the office and away from the desk regularly, daily.

Far better than an open door policy, is a daily practice of accessibility. This simple practice is also just one more technique that enables a leader to keep his fingers on the pulse of his team.

There is a danger here though, that regular accessibility on your part may be seen by your supervisors as undermining their authority. Guard carefully against this. If staff come to me and complain about something their supervisor said or done, or question a decision made, my first response is always, "Have you discussed this with your supervisor?" If the answer is no, and they are uncomfortable with raising the issue themselves, I offer to set up a meeting. It is very important your supervisors are not threatened by the staff talking to you about work issues and they know you are supportive of them.

Being accessible is more than just making it possible for staff to approach you. You need to be approachable. Take the time to listen and question for clarification. Thank your staff for bringing concerns your way or highlighting issues. If the issue requires you to get an answer back to them, tell them when they can expect to hear back from you on it, and then make sure they do! If necessary, put a reminder in your scheduler.

This approachability connects you and works to build trust. It helps you understand different perspectives and can often give you a heads-up on issues that will demand your attention. It breaks down barriers to communication.

Accessibility and approachability; personally I can't say enough how much I value it in those above me in the organization. I see it as a pre-requisite for effective management at all levels.

RULE #12
DON'T BUTT HEADS WITH CULTURE

Rarely has any leader been effective at altering cultural norms by saying *"From now on, we are going to think different and act different."* This is what I refer to as butting heads with culture.

This rule is all about establishing big changes in a workplace and doing it in such a way that the changes stick! You see, the bigger and older an organization is, the more ingrained is the culture. Cultural changes therefore are Big Changes and there's a catch phrase out there that says culture conquers change every day; or something like that. Yet changes in a workplace's culture do happen. If culture is so anchored and unmovable, how do those changes come about?

The answer is to not butt heads with it but to work with it. Help others recognize the culture they are in and the needs to, or benefits of making an adjustment. Provide them with examples of what change looks like. Help them see what change means to them and others, and then empower them to make the change.

The first part of this answer lies in the definition of culture. I define workplace culture as the activities and processes "held in place" by group attitudes. The second part of this answer is, culture isn't changed, it's influenced, and properly influenced, it changes itself.

Far more than simply changing a process, bringing about a change in a group's culture is the natural offshoot of a shift in their attitude. And attitudes do not shift without at least three things; information, example, and empowerment.

Take flat screen televisions for example. Our culture has shifted to these being the norm rather than the old cathode-ray style of television. When flat screens first came out, they were expensive and I, like so many others, was quite happy with my old TV. I mean why bother getting rid of a perfectly good TV right? Just because it weighed 300+ lbs and I couldn't move it without help, that's no reason to part with it.

Then I began noticing flat screens more and more in the stores, and some of my friends made the change. I was definitely impressed by the high definition pictures I seen in the store displays and I noted the prices were coming down. I began seeing them more and more in friends and neighbor's houses, and I was influenced by all this.

Do you see the process; how our culture shifted to flat screens being the norm? First we all heard they were out there... *information*. Then we seen them in stores; different styles and sizes and learned about LCDs verses

Plasma Screens etc.... *more information.* Then we began seeing them in friend's and neighbor's houses... *examples.* And wonder of wonders, they became affordable... *empowerment.*

This process has happened thousands of times and is happening right now to all of us.

Now bringing this back to the workplace, you can see that if you need to influence the culture, it starts with information rather than directives. Your staff need to understand what's out there. What's driving the need for change? What's the problem? You need to provide examples or illustrate the value of making a change as well as the impact of not making it. You need to empower and then support them as the change comes about.

Even if you know exactly what the change entails, you still need to first convey the need or reasons behind the change. Then show what that change looks like and make sure your staff know you are prepared to do what you need to in supporting them to make the change.

"People don't resist change.
They resist being changed"
~Peter Senge ~

A workplace's culture is held in place by individuals that don't see any reason or need to change. Sometimes it's everyone, which leads to stagnation unless there's an intervention of some sort, but more often, it's just a handful of employees.

One of your first challenges as a new manager is to determine who holds your team's culture in place; and I'm talking about those workplace leaders you can't pick off an org chart, but they are leaders none the less. They are part of the team. Their opinion is either valued or feared for a number of reasons and as a rule, the staff are usually just as interested in hearing what they have to say when you are not there, as when you are.

Curious enough, these cultural anchors that resist change and slow forward progress with the strength of their attitude or opinion, are also your greatest allies in bringing about a cultural change if you can figure out who they are and then get them on-side by communicating the problem and need for change If you can do this, things will start to move before your eyes.

Then there are also the cultural norms about how fast people work verses how fast they are expected to work; how long they are supposed to take for coffee verses how long they actually take. When are they supposed to stop for lunch verses when they actually stop?

Now if you work in a factory where the bell rings, the assembly line starts and everyone needs to be in their places, this is a mute point. Start and stop times, coffee breaks, and work pace are established. Performance is assessed on the absence of errors, line stoppage, and product consistency.

But more people don't work in factories than do. For them, there is rarely a bell at the start and end of coffee break and performance standards are established by industry norms and the expectations of coworkers, management and clients. Punch clocks do nothing for productivity and don't guarantee start and stop times. They only confirm presence.

In these scenarios, cultural norms require thoughtful observation. Do they hinder productivity? Are there safety aspects to consider? Are they reflective of morale? What is the impact of working to change them? How to change them? And once changed, what controls need to be in place to prevent them from migrating back to the old way?

Hours mean nothing!
There's activity and there's productivity.
Shoot for the latter.

I would like to introduce here, the concept of a balanced consideration in how you address cultural norms of this sort. For example, you may set a goal for yourself of pinning coffee breaks down to exactly the ten or fifteen minutes allotted but in doing so, you may also be negatively affecting moral and productivity.

To illustrate this, I know of one manager whose practice was to join her staff for coffee, and at exactly the 15 minute point, she would stand up and make her way slowly to the door, and if everyone wasn't on their way to the door by the time she got there, she would look at them and wait until they were on their feet and moving. The moral in that team was low. The trust levels were low and frustrations were high.

Reminders are fine, and in some situations they need to be quite firm, but the result in this example, of being a visible daily time keeper eroded the morale of her team and they seen it as the absence of trust, which it may well have been.

My experience is, moral is linked to productivity; and trusting your team makes them trustworthy. Everything is connected.

As for how fast people work verses how fast they are expected to work. The balanced approach here starts with not making assumptions but going and talking to the employee(s). Does he know what pace is expected; or the impact of tardiness? You've noticed that things are taking longer than usual, is everything alright? Has something changed that you are unaware of?

Now there are individual performance management issues that will invariably crop up from time to time, especially with a larger workforce. But more often than not, a timely and appropriate conversation will not only eliminate the need for discipline, but work to build a better relationship between you and the employee. At the very least, he will be aware you are aware.

How everything ties together is what is important here. As long as productivity is not hampered and unsafe conditions are not created, a good supervisor or manager will not interfere. But the moment team productivity is an issue, he has to step in and the best place to start is usually with those unofficial leaders on the team. Unsafe conditions will also command his attention with the individuals involved.

As manager, you need to ensure your supervisors understand their role in this and that they can call on you when needed.

So in your communications to bring about change, paying a little extra attention to the unofficial leaders has never hurt. Change their negative or past behaviors and the rest of the team will follow. Any individual on the crew that continuously opposes the supervisor and refuses to modify negative behaviour needs to be dealt with quickly and decisively if improvements to productivity or safety are to be achieved. Believe me, the rest of your team are waiting to see what happens to him!

Recognize and appreciate those involved in moving your team forward personally and publicly, directly and indirectly. And by indirectly, I'm talking about praising their actions to others when they are not around. Others will then know you will speak of their positive contributions as well.

Influencing culture is similar to teaching. It is impossible to teach someone something they have no interest in learning unless you are first able to help them see the value and need for the lesson. It is impossible to bring about a change in culture (attitude) if folks don't see the value or need for a change. If someone is motivated to learn, you have only to provide them with the information. If people see the value in, and need for a cultural shift or a change in perspective; you have only to demonstrate what it looks like.

If people see something positive in a change of attitude, it can happen overnight.

So if the culture of a workplace is held in place by attitude. It can still pivot on awareness. That is your key. By positively affecting staff's attitude, and raising their awareness, you influence the culture. By engaging your staff, specifically the unwritten leaders, and by drawing on their history and knowledge of the place to help solve problems; you affect their perspective and incrementally adjust the culture.

Spread throughout this book, are many other ways whereby you as a manager, influence the culture of your workplace. i.e. Tell yourself the right stories, place trust first, put yourself in their shoes, don't let your ego make decisions, recognize the value and competencies of your staff, own your mistakes… and the list goes on. Before long, my hope is you will be able to add more ways of your own to this list.

RULE #13

DON'T SOLVE PROBLEMS YOURSELF

Something that has never failed to impress me is the problem solving ability of a team. Even the smallest team of two will, by collaborating, come up with options and solutions that neither of them would have come up with on their own.

So again, whether you are a manager or supervisor, when faced with a problem to solve, this is a leadership moment and your staff are often your best source of options and solutions. Pull some of your people together and lay the problem out for them so they understand why it's a problem and the importance of finding a workable solution.

Once they understand why it's a problem and the importance of, or value in fixing it; they'll often come up with options you would have never thought of.

I would be remiss at this point if I didn't also point out that how you handle their suggestions will determine if you get any more from them. This doesn't mean you should undertake every suggestion or even that all their suggestions will be good ideas. What I do mean is, even when something seems at first, to be a bad idea, there can be some value in exploring it. Sometimes a bad idea contains the elements of the solution. Bottom line is, if your staff get the impression you aren't listening or that their suggestions aren't valued by you, you probably won't hear much from them in the future.

The best part of problem solving with your staff is not that they will come up with workable solutions, which they almost always will, but that they co-own the solution with you and each other. It is their idea! They want to solve it. Lets face it, we are all problem solvers at heart. Your role is to work with them in coming up with the best option to choose in solving the problem and then empowering them to bring it about. Back this up with well placed and deserved recognition and you have a problem solving machine.

"Perpetuity decisions are a trap. Avoid the dead-hand control."

In the days of sailing ships, in an emergency, lashing the rudder enabled seamen to attend to other more pressing things like saving the ship or themselves. They called it "dead-hand control" and the moment the emergency passed, a live hand resumed control of the ship.

Today however, for many organizations, processes and/or policies are established and then just left in place.

Like a forgotten "dead-hand control." If you are a new manager, you will be seeing these things for the first time. Your fresh eyes may see opportunities that have been right in front of others for so long, they didn't recognize them.

After observing the Six-month rule of Chapter 1, and you have an understanding of why things are the way they are, this is the time to address the opportunities. In addition to this, after having been with the company for much longer than six months, it is quite likely you will still come across scenarios where, when questioned, the answer you'll get is, "Oh we've always done that.", or some version of this.

This type of an answer should be an instant flag for you, and I would recommend a closer look. The word "Always" means either they aren't aware there is a new or better way of doing something (and there may not be), or they aren't interested in changing.

If they simply haven't explored an improvement in that particular area, it is a good time to bring your problem solving machine into play.

"After you've done a thing the same way for two years, look it over carefully. After five years, look at it with suspicion. And after ten years, throw it away and start all over."

-- Alfred Edward Perlman~
New York Times, 1958

After allowing for some healthy skepticism, if you sense there is no interest at all in change or improvement, you are now likely dealing with a cultural roadblock and so in addition to laying out the problem for them, be prepared to provide them with more information and examples of what's possible, potential benefits, etc. and empower them. This of course, is laid out in the previous chapter.

"Silence is a tool of engagement"

One last point I'll make on enlisting the help of others in problem solving, is about the effectiveness of silence. As a technique to engage others in problem solving, silence is quite effective. As a manager and leader, you should know the power of silence.

You see, people will love the silence of the wilderness, and value the quiet in a library, but will feel some pressure to fill the silence after a question. I suppose extraverts may feel this pressure more than introverts, but all feel it. So when you ask a question of your team or staff, wait for an answer. Don't fill that silence yourself unless it is to rephrase the question.

If you want to see this work, at your next staff meeting, ask for a volunteer for some job, and then clam up and wait. Unless it's a really terrible thing you're asking someone to do, someone will always break the silence. If it is a distasteful task, it will usually take just a little longer.

I worked for an expert at this silent leverage. She would take the time at a meeting to explain a course of action that was necessary to the organization and at the point where she had everyone's heads nodding like those little dogs in a car's back window, she would sit back in her chair and say, *"Unfortunately I don't have the time to set this up. If someone else would like to take this on, I can steer them in the right direction and be a resource to them?"* and then she would sit quiet and wait.

Only once did it happen that no-one spoke up, so after a few minutes, she just said, *"OK, well I guess we'll have to look for some other way."* and left the issue unsolved for want of someone to step up.

Before that meeting was over, another manager volunteered one of his staff, who wasn't at the meeting, for the job.

As an amusing side note, there was another guy in this building that employed the same tactic. It was entertaining to observe these two at the same meeting.

RULE #14

WORK WITH THE UNION

Here's what you as a manager want. You want your staff to see themselves as a team and each individual to know he or she is treated fairly. You want them to understand the importance of the work they do and that they are valued for their efforts. You want them feeling involved and empowered in so far as the work and the workplace enables. When you achieve this, your staff are most likely to come to work invested and engaged and there will be very few distractions to prevent them from achieving amazing results.

Unfortunately not all employees see themselves as members of a team like this, and it takes perseverance on your part as their manager to bring this about.

Now think about what the union wants. They want to see adherence to the collective bargaining agreement. They want members that know they are treated fairly and that work well with each other for the betterment of all. They too see the value of satisfied members that are empowered and invested. Whatever issues do come up, they want them resolved quickly and satisfactorily.

In this light, they also recognize that disciplinary measures are occasionally necessary when an employee's performance in the workplace is obviously out of line. Their role in this is to ensure whatever discipline does happen is fair, is based on performance, and is in accordance with the bargaining agreement.

What they don't want is to have to continuously and repeatedly defend that same employee whose workplace performance is culpable and obviously out of line.

The best way to understand this is to imagine yourself in the shoes of a union steward. Imagine yourself having to regularly argue in defense of the same employee simply because that's your job as a shop steward. Now if the employee was being wronged in some way, that's different. But there are many times when you know that the manager has a point, but you still have to argue for leniency and challenge any discipline because that's your job.

In other situations, there is no right or wrong and you find yourself in one of those grey zones where every answer starts with, "that depends..." And then there's the times when after a number of meetings, the employee negates all the ground you've gained on his behalf with a single thoughtless comment. It sounds emotionally draining doesn't it.

Now imagine yourself the union rep in a work place where the employees are treated fairly, involved, empowered, recognized and engaged. You might not be very busy as a shop steward in a place like this, but when you are called upon, the problems brought to your attention will be real, reasonable, and beneficial in that their solution will make the workplace better. Now there's some job satisfaction for you.

At the end of the day, you as a manager might be approaching issues from a different perspective than the union, but in the big picture, you both want the same thing.

So what does working <u>with</u> the union look like? Very simple, level with them, tell them what the problem is, and why it's a problem. Talk about things like impact on the workplace and on other members, and throughout all of this, and this is the most important part, be honest with your self about what you really want; what your intent is.

Here is where it can be the most difficult and the most rewarding to check your ego at the door. (See Rule 15) Recognize that part of you that's pushing for discipline is just your ego. And if you remove the ego, the manager that remains just wants the negative behaviour to stop and productivity to resume.

Once the union reps in your work place see that you are focused on the behaviour, and not the individual, they too begin talking behaviour, and the comments around the table at either an investigative or disciplinary meeting are focused on helping the employee understand the problem and the importance of its resolution.

I've actually had Union Reps. point out to employees at meetings like this that a continuation of their behaviour will lead to stronger discipline, which is usually a point made by management.

Once the union realizes you are earnest in being fair to employees and genuinely interested in making the workplace better by resolving problems, everyone wins.

What is critical to keep in mind here is that the need to separate the performance from the person is often overlooked. Your job as a manager is to do exactly this every time you have a meeting to address an employee performance issue, disciplinary or not.

Separate the performance from the individual and focus on the performance. If any of your employees performed in the same manner, it would be the same issue. It is the performance you need corrected. There can be no personality involved in the positive resolution of a performance problem. It is not a personal issue between you and the employee, for that would be all ego based. Once you decide you are not taking things personally and you check you ego at the door, all that is left is addressing acceptable verses unacceptable behaviour.

This is not always easy however. During employee performance meetings, as much as your focus and comments are directed at unacceptable behaviour or performance, you may find yourself dealing with a defense by the union based on how you as a manager have failed in some way. I.e. You never said something at the right time; or you never made expectations clear to the employee; or you allowed someone else to do it; or you haven't provided training...

It can be an exhausting list to defend against but the point is, don't take it personally! But do take it seriously enough to prepare by anticipating the arguments, and if possible have documented answers at the meeting. Documentation is your friend. i.e.:

➤ **"Yes, I told him this and both he and Joe were present."**

➤ **"We've discussed this before on these dates......"**

➤ **"The employee has proven his ability to do this job before. Here are examples,,, so no training is required."**

➤ **Here are statements from other employees (or clients) describing his behaviour.**

➤ **Here is the summary of our last meeting regarding this behaviour, and here is the letter sent to...**

Another reason I say don't take things personally is; unions can be, and are charged by their own members, and fined for not putting forth a sufficient defense. I've had three different union stewards state outright at meetings that it doesn't matter what I say, they are being paid to disagree with me. To be honest, this took me a while to wrap my head around but it's true.

Their members need to see them as raising any and every possible defense against discipline and in favour of leniency if discipline is involved.

So with that recognition of the principle affecting their actions, I began to see their comments as a sort of explanation as to why they wouldn't agree even though they could see the reasonableness of points raised. It was a little confusing, but eventually I've gotten to the point where neither party were taking things personally, and we were able to focus on "what acceptable behaviour looked like" and the situations were satisfactorily resolved.

Here are four managerial mindsets, that if adopted and applied, will go a long way in convincing union reps you want to work "with them" to solve workplace issues.

If you make a mistake, (and we all do on occasion), own it! The moment you are aware of it, clean it up without making the union initiate a grievance process. If you or one of your supervisors called in the wrong guy on overtime, you ensure the guy that should have been called gets paid. Let the union know a mistake was made and you are making it right, and if they are the ones bring your attention to the error, thank them.

Think first to give individuals the benefit of the doubt before moving to discipline. (Remember believing is seeing from Rule #9) More often than not, there is more to the situation than you initially know. Open and upfront communication is the key here.

Remember that performance problem solving rarely means dismissal, and you don't need to be the only one coming up with solutions. The employee can, and so can the union. On many occasions, I've identified problems to union reps along with a proposed course of action; only to have them counter with an alternate course of action. Albeit, it is usually less drastic, the ensuing discussion usually ensures everyone understands the problem and outcome desired. They have an obligation to defend their members, but reasonableness rules the day when culpable behavior is involved.

Don't be afraid of grievances. Some grievances are good. You want them. Grievances and their resolution are excellent problem solving tools that bring letters of understanding into effect, documenting solutions to systemic problems, and here again, you and the union are working together to make a better workplace.

RULE #15

CHECK YOUR EGO
AT THE DOOR

I've been using this line at work for years, but in reality, it applies to every door you walk through. This is one of those rules that weaves its way through and harmonizes with all the other rules. Our egos, if unrecognized and unchecked can, and often do get us in trouble.

If you have just been promoted to manager; good for you and congratulations, go ahead and feel good about this. It's right and normal to feel good about the recognition that goes along with a promotion. You should appreciate your family is proud of you but guard against letting self-pride gain a foothold in you.

The difference between feeling good about a promotion and being proud in your new role is this. If you feel good, you'll not be concerned that others see the challenges you face in your new role, and folks will work with you and give you a hand. If pride gets in the way however, you'll find yourself trying to hide the challenges you face, from those around you; basically shutting yourself off from their support.

By checking your ego at the door and not letting pride influence your thoughts, questions, or answers; any and all feedback you get will be food for thought. However, if pride gets in the way; then the opinions of others will be taken too personally. Compliments will seem justified and complaints will feel like personal criticisms. In essence, your pride will be enabling those around you to control your mood and your responses.

For example, if you feel personally offended when someone suggests there is a better way to do something, it is your ego getting in the way. Without your ego clouding your thoughts, you would objectively consider the suggestion and either go with it or discard it for logical reasons. We've all seen a perfect example of this in Science Officer Spock.

"Move on without hanging on."

So be aware that pride is one of those potholes in the road big enough to knock you off course. If you make a mistake, you've also learned a lesson. If you made a mistake yesterday, be glad you are aware of it today. If things don't go as you hoped they would, figure out why and plan for next time. Move on without hanging on to the negatives of yesterday. By hanging onto the negatives, you are undermining your own confidence and ability. So file the mistakes and apply the lessons and for goodness sake, don't let your ego stop you from sharing with others what you've learned the hard way or from asking for help when you need it.

There is no better place to check your ego at the door, then at staff meetings. A manager's best opportunity to communicate with staff is at staff meetings. This is where I usually introduce the concept to new managers. Whether you have staff meetings weekly, bi-weekly, every morning, or once a month, your goal should always be, to be real with your staff; no pretenses. And in so doing, create a setting where staff are free to raise whatever workplace issues are concerning them; even if they are upset with you.

Good staff meetings don't happen by accident. Like every good meeting, there should be ground rules and three rules I recommend managers establish for staff meetings are:

- ➤ Check your ego at the door.
- ➤ You can raise any issue you like, just find a respectful way to say it.
- ➤ If you raise a problem, be prepared to offer a possible solution as well.

These three rules make for productive meetings.

I usually reinforce the second rule with the first by telling the staff I won't take the things they say to me personally. And here's the trick. If you as manager, are challenged, your task, first and foremost, is to understand what your employee's perception of things is, that he or she would think their comments to you are justified. What has she seen or heard, where is the misunderstanding? Once you understand where they are coming from, you will bring understanding to the room without having lost your temper or evading the issue. And you will have gone a long way towards building the trust that makes for a great team.

(Note: This rule goes hand in hand with Rule #5, the staff needing to see your "Calm")

"Who's more important, you or I?"

Sam Walton, the founder of Walmart said, "The best leader is the servant leader." As their manager, the stronger your focus is on this and the harder you work for your staff to ensure they have what they need to do the job, the stronger and more competent as a team they will be, which in turn makes you a better manager.

So here is a balance point to consider. As manager, on one side you have the organization's goals and deadlines to meet. On the other side you have to know and meet the needs of your staff. The interesting point is, in order to meet the needs on one side; you have to meet the needs of the other.

> **"Nearly all men can stand adversity, but if you want to test a man's character, give him power."**
> **~Abraham Lincoln~**

I like to relate my role as manager to employees this way. I point out the difference between them taking a day off and me taking a day off. If they are absent, something doesn't get done, the organization is impacted; and I need to replace them if I am to minimize the impact of their absence. Whereas, if I take a day off, there is no impact at the front line, or at least there shouldn't be. The organization doesn't come to a halt and our clients continue to receive the services we provide.

I ask them, "So who's more important, you or I?" Then I point out that we all have a job to do and my job is simply to make sure they have everything they need to do their jobs. As a manager, by seeing this as your role, you are ensuring your staff have the best chance of meeting the organization's goals and deadlines.

RULE #16

DON'T TAKE THINGS PERSONALLY

Of all the rules, this can be one of the toughest to stay with. This might seem a repeat of "Checking Your Ego at the Door," and it is definitely in the same category, but I single it out because there is a big difference.

Remember, you're the boss, and deserved or not, when your staff aren't happy, regardless the reason, they will often see it as your fault or at least partly your fault, simply because you are the boss. Sooner or later, you are bound to run into this and when you do, don't take it personally, but recognize it is simply human nature in the workplace.

The honest feedback you want from your staff is usually from a singular perspective; theirs. If you are going to be a good manager, you need to understand their perspective; where their comments and opinions are coming. You don't need to agree, but you should strive to understand.

You see, now we are talking about opinions based on values, culture, personal likes and dislikes. This is different from sorting out a misunderstanding as I mentioned in the last chapter. This level of understanding is much bigger and broader in scope.

Your goal again, is to try and understand their point of view, where they are coming from and what their fears or hopes are.

"Figure out the underlying reason."

Keep in mind, each of your staff come from different back grounds, have different personal values, have different goals, have a personal perspective of what's important that will likely differ in some way from each of your other staff. They each have a personal life. All these things affect them at work.

So this rule isn't about you sorting out other people's misunderstandings, it's about understanding your staff and the singular perspective of each brings to the workplace. Then filtering what you see and hear through that understanding. If you are a new manager or have some new crew members, you haven't had time to get to know them, but you can still use your understanding of differences to keep you from taking things personally.

This rule applies in your dealings with those that report to you, that work alongside you, and that you take direction from.

Some simple examples of considering where people are coming from are:

1. I once picked up some lumber at a lumber yard. This particular lumber yard was right next door to its competition, another lumber yard. The young man that helped me load the truck grabbed a red flag out of a box and stapled it to the long boards sticking out of the back of my truck. I noticed it was the competition's red flag, and pointed it out to him. His answer was, "Look, I'm not making a career out of this, this is just a summer job, I could care less whose flag it is."

   This young guy met the need for the safety flag as he was trained, but he wasn't focused on advertising, or perhaps he never seen the wording on the flag as important since it was un-readable in the wind anyway. The concept that his boss wouldn't want him supporting the competition in this manner wouldn't even have occurred to him; totally understandable.

2. I once had a fellow from Ecuador working for me in a machine shop. He had only been there a few weeks, and I had given him a large conveyor assembly to do. It was taking a long time and I realized it was easier done by two people. So I grabbed some tools and helped him. It went much faster with two sets of hands working together and we were done by the end of the day.

Now normally he was friendly and talkative, but during this time and afterward, I noticed he was less talkative, and a little sullen. I learned from him later that even though I explained my reason for giving him a hand, he saw my assistance as a sign of displeasure with his work. You see, in Ecuador, in the factory he came from, the supervisor never worked with the men. My reassurance that all was ok was trumped by his cultural perspective that it wasn't.

3. This last example to illustrate the importance of not taking things personally and recognizing where people are coming from is about a departmental restructuring that I was involved in. It resulted in a position being created between my boss and I, so that I no longer reported to him. Now one could easily take this personally in a number of negative ways, but in this case, it wasn't about me, but my director. You see, he had fourteen different departmental managers reporting to him on the activities of 600 – 700 staff. In addition to this, he was involved in a number of other corporate initiatives; with the end result being, he was just spread too thin. It was just too much and he was unable to find enough time in the week to give each of the managers the time they needed.

These examples illustrate how easily you as a manager can encounter scenarios that, if you are not on your guard, might take personally. They can come at you from your staff, your peers or your supervisor, and unless you take the time to fill in the gaps in your own understanding, you might respond inappropriately, initiating a chain reaction of events.

The last point here is an echo of what I've said in the last chapter. Just as you might misunderstand and take things personally, so can others. This is why I advise, when you are challenged on something; your goal is to find out what their perspective is that makes them feel their comments are justified. They may simply have a different perspective, or they may have taken something personally.

RULE #17

ASSUME CONNECTIONS EXIST

Watch for and make note of connections. If none are readily apparent, still assume they exist somewhere. Between your staff, your coworkers, upper management, your suppliers, your competitors, your neighbors, and your friends; they are there somewhere, even if they don't jump out.

Who's related to whom? Who's on the same hockey team? Who coaches whose kid? Who used to work with who? Who are neighbors, and who are workplace buddies, etc. As with getting to know your organization, this too will take time, especially if you are new to an organization; but knowing these connections is the political component of the big picture you ultimately want to have an understanding of.

It is after all, a political world. People know people!

One of my favorite examples to drive home the point of, "it's a political world" comes from an experience in government where every summer my staff numbers were bolstered with the addition of a few summer students here and there. They would be hired to do grounds work or be cleaners, etc.

And every summer, there would be a number of inquiries from a higher level of government requiring me to look into a situation because an off-hand comment made around the lunch table at work would be repeated out of context at home by one of the students.

You see, the government received hundreds of applicants for a relatively few number of summer positions. Now perhaps it was because of how the applications were filled out, such as preference of where to work, or available start and ending times, or willingness to work shift work. Or perhaps it was because of related studies, or previous experience, I can't say; but what did impress me is the percentage of these students that knew or who's references were from someone else in Government.

It happened on a few occasions, when asked at home, "So how's your summer job going?" Some of their answers, after being in the job for just a few weeks, often painted a slightly different picture than reality.

One occasion of this resulted in an inquiry that started with, "It has come to our attention that the work load is not being equitably distributed at..."

In this particular example, an employee had apparently convinced the student, he was given more work to do than others and that was just not fair. The student went home and talked about favoritism in the workplace. There being just a few degrees of separation, this unacceptable situation made its way to a higher government office driving an inquiry.

Remember in Chapter three, I talked about not sending email hammered out in anger. If you are still tempted to send it, consider this. In customer service terms, I've heard that if one gets good service from a company, they will tell five or six other people over the next few months. But if one gets terrible service or is mistreated, they will share that with way more than twenty people and will remember the bad service or treatment for the next 20 years.

Now apply that to an angry email and the fact that connections exist.

So why is it important to assume connections exist? It simply helps you understand the workplace better and heightens the importance and value of thinking before speaking and strategic communication.

RULE #18

PLACE TRUST FIRST

"We awaken in others the same attitude
of mind we hold toward them."
~Elbert Hubbard~

Before your staff can trust you, you need to trust them. This doesn't come naturally to some, and is a skill to be developed, but it is a fact that staff in general will live up to or down to your expectations. (See "Work your Attitude")

If you demonstrate trust in your staff, and they feel it; they will generally work to keep it. So start in your new role by placing trust in your staff first rather than by requiring them to earn it. Let them feel your trust and they will naturally understand their ability loose it.

Rarely does it happen that you will not strive to live up to the trust someone has in you. This applies to your staff too. If you have an individual or two that cannot be trusted, they will soon identify themselves through their actions.

"The only way to make a man
trustworthy is to trust him."
~Henry L. Stimson~

I have increased the signing authority of every one of my supervisors and assistant managers in the last decade and not one of them has abused the heightened authority. In fact, it has been operationally expedient in many cases to assign a number of front line staff some signing authority as well and the same holds true. They haven't let their supervisors or me down, not once!

Placing trust first can be challenging for a new manager whose orientation can often be full of all the horror stories of the past. Make no mistake, having the history of events and staff is valuable, but your arrival is a new beginning, for them and you. The turn-over you receive can colour your perspective and as a new manager you will naturally be on "full receive." But filter what you hear; from everyone, including your boss.

"If you look for the bad in people
expecting to find it, you surely will."
~Abraham Lincoln~

It's interesting that whenever you hear people talk about getting organized, they are usually not talking about organizing their thinking. Yet this is the key to working with people. It affects how you view them, communicate with them, support them or discipline them for what you perceive to be culpable behavior

The best and easiest way to place trust first is by telling yourself the right story as I mentioned in Chapter 8. It might sound naïve, but just know that no-one intentionally does a bad job. Expect the best from everyone.

Soon after moving into the position of manager, you should take the time to clarify the working relationship you require with your supervisors. Ensure they know the types of things you expect to be notified about and those things you trust them to handle without involving you. The decisions you expect them to make and the decisions you need to be informed of, may seem obvious, but a discussion around these things eliminates the, "Oh I didn't realize..." conversation later. Anything they are unsure of, they can bring to you.

Keep two things in mind when you plan out these conversations.

➢ This is their first opportunity to <u>feel</u> the trust you place in them and this may be the first time your supervisors have had a discussion like this with any manager.

➢ You are establishing the balance between the autonomy you need them to have and exercise; and the awareness you need, to manage the operation.

Promote ownership in your staff

You want staff that know they are (or could be), key components of the operation. And even though they are part of something much bigger than themselves, they own their part.

As a manager, you should be appreciating and appraising the levels of ownership and attitude evidenced by your staff's performance. Wherever you find ownership and attitude lacking, this is an indicator of where you need to devote some attention. This, for me, is a higher priority than devoting time to various skill sets. An employee with a great attitude and few skills can be supported into a great career. Whereas an employee with great skills but a terrible attitude will rarely stop being problematic. So many times I have seen and heard of people hired for their skill and fired for their attitude.

**Few things help an individual more than
to place responsibility upon him, and to
let him know that you trust him.**
~Booker T. Washington~

The topic of ownership fits nicely into many discussions you will have with your staff. Ownership starts when employees know they make a difference and have received recognition for it from either the clients, their supervisors, or best of all, both. When employees feel ownership of the job they do, they are also more likely to give you their honest opinion about things, and this is what you want. When a team of employees take ownership of a job and know what they do is important, morale and productivity goes up and absenteeism goes down.

At the end of the day, if you believe the best of your staff, you will see the best in your staff. And with very few exceptions, it has been my experience that staff will return the trust you place in them.

RULE #19

OWN YOUR JOB

I guess the best way to explain this rule is to consider where you and your boss are in the organization. Put your self in your boss's shoes. What does he or she need from you? What did he or she get from your predecessor? What's changed? You can use these questions to flesh out your job description.

For example, I had been in one particular management role for just a few months when I started hearing from my director almost weekly, about how frustrated he was with a situation where, for one reason or another, and through no fault of their own, certain of my staff weren't addressing a recurring situation fast enough to prevent numerous complaints from coming to him in email or on his cell. This situation had been an ongoing concern when I joined the team and there were numerous factors involved besides the actions of my staff. For me though, the message was fairly clear, he had been frustrated with this situation for some time.

I knew the first thing needed was essentially for these problems to disappear off his radar screen, i.e. clear away this source of frustration, and that was my job!

So I focused on equipping and empowering the staff to address the recurring situation and organizing them to be in the right place at the right time. I had heard so many different opinions of the problem that I made sure I was there myself on several occasions to understand the issues first hand and to talk with the staff about this particular customer service aspect of their jobs. From there, I assessed training needs and provided as required. Through it all, I communicated the need for speed, and recognized them for their truly excellent work as they began nipping things in the bud and solving the issues that had been causing problems.

Six months later, that same director commented, "Things have sure been quiet. There haven't been any issues brought to my attention for a long time." I silently filed that as an achievement!

To really understand your role in the organization, consider the answers you might have if asked questions such as:

> ➤ What all have you changed in the last year or two?
> ➤ What new processes have you initiated?
> ➤ How's the morale of your crew?
> ➤ What leadership competencies are you working on strengthening and why?
> ➤ How much are you delegating?

➢ Is the next training session you are planning for your staff?

➢ What changes do you see as necessary or beneficial and where are you in bringing them about?

➢ What's your plan to address the most frequent problems your staff encounter?

➢ Whom all are you coaching and mentoring to replace you?

You can't "own" your job if you don't fully grasp your role.

Another thing to consider in owning your job is again, your staff's perspective of things and their level of understanding regarding the decisions made that impact their jobs. What more information can you share with them so they are, "In the know"? Then ask yourself, "They need me to...... what?" (You fill in the blank)

There are a myriad of answers to this question, but they will all add up in some way to just a few points.

Firstly, your staff need you to make sure they have what they need to do their job safely and efficiently. Whether it be tools, training or simply your attention, they will let you know what they need either intentionally or unintentionally. i.e. If they need more training, they will let you know it either verbally or through their performance. If they need more specific direction than you are providing, or more of your direct attention, they'll let you know the same way.

Secondly, your staff need to know you take your job (and theirs) seriously and part of this is representing them and their interests as best you can. When things don't go well, they need to know you have done what you could as their manager. You are their best source to confirm or deny rumors. (I often like to lead off a staff meeting with, "So has anyone heard any good rumours?")

Thirdly, your staff (just like your Director) need you to think about and plan for the future; i.e. making sure your department has the manpower and skill sets it needs to do tomorrow's job is your job today. If the skills needed are going to change, you have to be ahead of the game, or the team will flounder when the time comes. They need to hear from you, about your goals for the team and why. They need to hear from you what their role is in meeting those goals and what your expectations of them are.

Make no mistake, this isn't a popularity contest. Managers that are afraid to upset their staff will fail to make the hard decisions when necessary. They will waffle and waiver and delay until the matter is taken out of their hands. They won't confront poor performers or hold others accountable. They won't question openly, why something is always done the same old way, and the department or organization's performance suffers as a result.

As a new manager, you have that distinct advantage of being that needed new set of eyes that see things for the first time, whereas everyone else has been looking at it for so long, they don't see it anymore. So take advantage of your newness in the position to question what you see.

"You Move First."

As a manager, owning your job means you are always in the position of, "You Move First." Keeping Rule 1 for new managers in mind (Make no Changes for Six Months), once you are passed the six month point, this aspect of owning your job is all about taking the time to think and plan. Take the time to consider short term needs; long term goals; service delivery status and challenges, industry changes, staff development needs, corporate changes and impacts. By spending time thusly, you are often able to make the changes before the changes are forced upon you; introduce before being introduced; solve before questions are posed; and ready yourself and/ or your staff for changes to come.

The last part of owning your job is to be organized. Owning your job is a thousand times easier if you are organized. Unfortunately there are a number of ways people are "organized" so let's define "organized".

I know a guy with a desk buried under stacks of paper. He has a coffee can jammed full of pens and pencils and no apparent place on his desk to lay a sheet of paper to write on. I know another guy who abhors any paper on his desk other than the one he is working with at the moment. His office always looks like it was just dusted, (*and it might have been too*). Both of these fellows are organized! I know because I can walk into their office and ask either of them for a specific report, or the minutes of a meeting, or a certain spreadsheet, and each will know exactly where it is, pull it out from a stack or out of a file and there is no searching involved.

These guys represent both ends of a scale. I know lots of folks in the middle of this scale that are not organized, and could easily spend half an hour looking for a particular document. So here's my definition of being organized.

"Everything has a place,
And you know where it is".

If your boss comes into your office and asks for anything in your office, can you put your fingers on it? If so, then you're organized and kudos are due. If however, you lose things every so often, the same can't be said and it is worth your while to get organized; on your own time if necessary. Once you're organized, stay organized.

RULE #20

FORGET THE 40-HOUR WORK WEEK
(and keep your balance)

Let me say out loud right now; forget the 40 hour work week but don't loose your balance. As a manager, you are likely not getting paid by the hour but by the month. You are being paid to shoulder the responsibility for not only your work but the work of others. With the transition to management, most move from an hourly wage to a monthly salary to do a job whether it takes you 40 hours a week or 60 hours a week.

Now before you go thinking all you have to do is delegate and be organized in order to put in a 30 hour work week, let me also point out that coming in late and leaving early won't be viewed favorably by your staff, your co-workers, or your boss. So if you are able to manage your department by putting in less than 40 hours a week, kudos to you. Now you can use your free time to plan for the future of your department by researching new methods and technologies, looking for ways to improve service or decrease downtime, raise profits, or tackling that problem that keeps coming up.

The time you are able to free up for yourself is an opportunity for growth; take advantage of it.

Regarding when to start work, I personally like to take my cues from my boss and peers, and even if my boss starts work at 6:AM every morning, I'd be lying if I said it didn't feel good to beat him to work on occasion.

As a manager, you should consider 40 hours a week as a minimum. This doesn't mean your home life and spare time have to continuously take a back seat to the responsibilities of the job. What it means is, make it your practice to get to work before your staff and be prepared to stay an extra half hour to an hour after they leave.

Coming in half an hour early gives you preparation time and sets a good example for those around you. And that time after your staff leave is quiet time for you. This quiet time enables you to address many things you simply haven't had time to during the day; finish the report, respond to email, review the budget... So take advantage of it!

Be assured, there will be times when you simply need to put in even more time, but watch this doesn't become the norm. This is the "keep your balance" part.

It is so easy to get caught in the trap of dealing with work email at home in the evenings, and on the weekend, or on your cell wherever you are.

In one job I had, the manager in the next office was consistently there an hour before me and I got there early. He stayed to put in even more hours after I left, and I stayed late. Another manager I know regularly put in twelve to fourteen hour days, and went home quite late two or three days a week. I had a boss that took his laptop so he could stay connected and respond to email while vacationing on the other side of the planet.

These are examples of burn-out regimes and the very rare individual can keep it up for the long term. (Even rarer is the spouse that will put up with it for any length of time.)

Forget the 40 hour work-week doesn't mean kill yourself with ridiculous hours. Consider the definition of a Manager …One who handles, controls, or directs the activities of others. If you find yourself putting in longer and longer hours you either need to delegate some of the work to your staff, or, if this isn't an option, you need to talk to your director about getting you some help.

If you have a large number of staff, the same thing applies. You may at some point, realize you can't do everything yourself and something's going to slip between the cracks. Again, this is the time to make a change. I've worked with people who conduct themselves with the attitude of, "I can handle anything they throw at me. And I don't complain." These people usually find themselves unable to maintain a healthy work/life balance. They shoulder more stress than necessary and it shows.

So think "balance" when it comes to; your time with family verses your hours at work, the amount of sleep you need verses what you get, the food and drink you might need verses what you ingest. Balance in all things will make you an excellent manager.

SUMMARY

As I considered how to summarize the contents of this book, I realized it is far more important for you to consider the overall sentiment of the book rather than any one particular point.

Granted, every different scenario may highlight the immediate importance of one rule over the others, but the overall sentiment of this book is the greatest value. That is, you work with and lead people, some of which will have leadership skills of their own. Each of those you work with will have their own perspectives, opinions, expectations, and needs, and the more tuned in to these you are, the more effective you are as a leader. The overall sentiment of this book speaks to having a functional disposition towards the role of a manager / leader.

As a manager, yours is a multiple role: manager, controller, organizer, approver, supporter, mentor, trainer, communicator, coordinator, facilitator, discipliner, time keeper, motivator, supervisor, investigator, administrator, enabler, strategist, planner, change agent..., and these all role up into leader. You might think you are demonstrating leadership by certain actions or how you deal with challenges, but the reality is, you demonstrate the leader you are by just walking onto your work place, by your every day demeanor, by the time you take for people, by your every action.

> **"Men imagine that they communicate their
> virtue or vice by overt actions and do not see that
> virtue or vice emit a breath every moment."**
> **~Ralph Waldo Emerson~**

At the start of this book, I mentioned our ability to learn from good and bad examples. I encourage you to think about the supervisors and managers you have and have had. Think about their different styles and habits. What worked for them and what didn't? How did you see others responding to them? Thus you begin examining the day to day lessons provided you and adding your own rules to those presented here.

If you have already started emulating the good leaders around you, good for you.

That's what it's all about....

ABOUT THE AUTHOR

Guy P. Fehr, RPA. FMP. has sixteen years experience in the private sector and twenty-four years experience in the public sector. His forty years experience includes Facility Management, Administration, Organizational Development, Project Delivery, Maintenance and Operations, Construction and the Trades, Mining, Contracting, Railroads, Retail, Warehousing, and Trucking. Throughout his career, Guy has made a study of the workplace leaders encountered and he has utilized the lessons learned in the coaching and mentoring of numerous supervisors and managers, honing their day to day leadership skills.

Currently, working with a team of roughly one hundred and forty staff, he oversees the maintenance and operations of a five million square foot portfolio comprised of twenty-one healthcare facilities.

Mr. Fehr has been married for forty years. He and his wife live in Saskatoon, Saskatchewan.

To contact Mr. Fehr regarding customized training programs for supervisors and managers, or for more information on the unwritten rules of workplace leadership, or to comment on the contents of "The Unwritten Rules"; go to:

www.theunwrittenrules-leadership.com